SandCastle™

Character Concepts

Keep Your Cool!

Kelly Doudna

Consulting Editor, Diane Craig, M.A./Reading Specialist

ABDO
Publishing Company

Published by ABDO Publishing Company, 4940 Viking Drive, Edina, Minnesota 55435.

Printed in the United States.

Credits
Edited by: Pam Price
Curriculum Coordinator: Nancy Tuminelly
Cover and Interior Design and Production: Mighty Media
Photo Credits: Digital Vision, Hemera, ShutterStock

Library of Congress Cataloging-in-Publication Data

Doudna, Kelly, 1963-
   Keep your cool! / Kelly Doudna.
     p. cm. -- (Character concepts)
   ISBN-13: 978-1-59928-736-2
   ISBN-10: 1-59928-736-6
   1. Self-control--Juvenile literature. I. Title.

BJ1533.D49D68 2007
179'.9--dc22
                                                                2006032278

SandCastle™ books are created by a professional team of educators, reading specialists, and content developers around five essential components—phonemic awareness, phonics, vocabulary, text comprehension, and fluency—to assist young readers as they develop reading skills and strategies and increase their general knowledge. All books are written, reviewed, and leveled for guided reading, early reading intervention, and Accelerated Reader® programs for use in shared, guided, and independent reading and writing activities to support a balanced approach to literacy instruction.

Let Us Know

SandCastle would like to hear your stories about reading this book. What is your favorite page? Was there something hard that you needed help with? Share the ups and downs of learning to read. We want to hear from you! To get posted on the ABDO Publishing Company Web site, send us e-mail at:

sandcastle@abdopublishing.com

SandCastle Level: Transitional

Keep Your Cool!

Your character is a part of who you are. It is how you act when you go somewhere. It is how you get along with other people. It is even what you do when no one is looking!

You show character by keeping your cool. You use self-control instead of getting too excited. You don't lose your temper. You don't yell at your grandmother!

Amanda goes shopping with her sister. She is excited, but she doesn't run off. Amanda uses self-control.

Paige finds a stuffed lion she likes. She doesn't yell that she wants it. She asks for it calmly. Paige keeps her cool.

Sara counts her money. She knows that she has 20 dollars to spend at the store. Sara will use self-control.

Tyler wants to play with his new toy. His mother tells him that he must wait until they are at home. Tyler takes a deep breath. He keeps his cool.

Jason is hungry. He wants to eat a snack right now. But he helps put the groceries in the car instead. Jason uses self-control.

Keep Your Cool!

Jenna and her dad
are going to do
some shopping.
Jenna's so excited
that she can't
stop hopping.

Shopping List

1. ~~~~~~~~~~~~~~~~~
   2. ~~~~~~~~~~~
3. ~~~~~~~~~~~~~~~~
   ~~~~~~~~~~~~~~~~~
5. ~~~~~~~~~~~~~~~~~
6. ~~~~~~~~~~~~~~
   7. ~~~~~~~~

MALL

Jenna yells to her dad that he walks too slow. There are seven stores where she wants to go.

Then Jenna remembers
that it's better to be quiet.
She'll have plenty of time
to find something and buy it.

Jenna stays calm and gets her shopping done. By keeping her cool, she's had a lot more fun!

Did You Know?

President Thomas Jefferson advised counting to 10 before speaking as a way to keep your cool. He also recommended counting to 100 if you were really angry.

Cartoon characters who can't keep their cool are often shown with steam coming out of their ears.

Stress balls are squishy balls that you squeeze in your hand. They can help you keep your cool, but they are also a good way to exercise the muscles in your hand.

Glossary

calm – quiet and peaceful.

cool – calm and unexcited.

excited – eager and looking forward to something.

groceries – food items bought from a store.

self-control – showing control of your feelings or actions.

About SandCastle™

A professional team of educators, reading specialists, and content developers created the SandCastle™ series to support young readers as they develop reading skills and strategies and increase their general knowledge. The SandCastle™ series has four levels that correspond to early literacy development in young children. The levels are provided to help teachers and parents select appropriate books for young readers.

Emerging Readers
(no flags)

Beginning Readers
(1 flag)

Transitional Readers
(2 flags)

Fluent Readers
(3 flags)

These levels are meant only as a guide. All levels are subject to change.

To see a complete list of SandCastle™ books and other nonfiction titles from ABDO Publishing Company, visit **www.abdopublishing.com** or contact us at: 4940 Viking Drive, Edina, Minnesota 55435 • 1-800-800-1312 • fax: 1-952-831-1632